HURRICANES

Art—
Best regards.
Stephen
Leatherman

Dedication To: Mr. Samuel H. Swint, Jr. of Southampton, New York who advises people
to prepare for the worst and pray for the best when it comes to hurricanes.

This edition published in 2008 by Voyageur Press, an imprint of MBI Publishing Company,
400 First Avenue North, Suite 300, Minneapolis, MN 55401 USA

Voyageur Press titles are also available at discounts in bulk quantity for industrial or sales-promotional use. For details write
to Special Sales Manager at MBI Publishing Company, 400 First Avenue North, Suite 300, Minneapolis, MN 55401 USA.

To find out more about our books, join us online at www.voyageurpress.com.

Library of Congress Cataloging-in-Publication Data
Leatherman, Stephen P.
Hurricanes : causes, effects, and the future / by Stephen P. Leatherman and Jack Williams.
p. cm.
Includes index.
ISBN 978-0-7603-2992-4 (sb : alk. paper)
1. Hurricanes. I. Williams, Jack, 1936- II. Title.
QC944.L43 2008
551.55'2—dc22
2008009851

Illustrations and Photography copyright © 2008 by:

Front Cover © NASA/Johnson Space Center
Back cover © FEMA/Robert Kaufmann
Page 1 © Corbis/epa/John Sevigny
Page 3 © FEMA/Robert Kaufmann
Page 4 © FEMA/Marty Bahamonde
Page 6 © NASA/Johnson Space Center
Page 8 © Corbis/UltimateChase/Mike Theiss
Page 9 © FEMA/Liz Roll
Page 10 © NASA/Visible Earth
Page 12/13 © Richard Garratt
Page 15 © NASA
Page 16 © FEMA/Marvin Nauman
Page 19 © Stephen Leatherman
Page 20 © FEMA/Jocelyn Augustino
Page 22 © FEMA/John Fleck
Page 25 © NOAA/Lt Mike Silah

Page 29 © NASA/Johnson Space Center
Page 30 © NASA/Visible Earth
Page 32 © NOAA
Page 34 © NASA/Johnson Space Center
Page 35 © RAINEX/Derek Ortt/John Cangialosi
Page 37 © NASA
Page 38 © FEMA/Bob McMillan
Page 41 © Richard Garratt
Page 43 © PA Photos/AP/Dave Martin
Page 45 left © PA Photos/AP/Eric Gay
Page 45 right © PA Photos/AP/Phil Coale
Page 46 © FEMA/Win Henderson
Page 47 © PA Photos/AP/Johnny Hanson
Page 48 © FEMA/Bob McMillan
Page 49 © FEMA/Robert Kaufmann
Page 50 © U.S. Library of Congress

Page 52 © Science Faction/Jim Reed
Page 53 © FEMA/Liz Roll
Page 55 © NASA/Visible Earth
Page 56 © NASA/Earth Observatory
Page 58/59 © Richard Garratt
Page 60 © Science Faction/Jim Reed
Page 61 © Corbis/epa/Alejandro Ernesto
Page 63 © NASA/Visible Earth
Page 64 © NASA/Johnson Space Center
Page 69 © FEMA/John Fleck
Page 70 left to right/top to bottom ©
FEMA/Jocelyn Augustino, Robert Kaufmann,
Jocelyn Augustino, Mark Wolfe,
Jocelyn Augustino, Mark Wolfe,
Jocelyn Augustino, John Fleck, Liz Roll,
Bob McMillan, Andrea Booher, Dave Gatley

Front cover: *Hurricane Elena, Gulf of Mexico, 1985.* Page 1: *Hurricane Rita hits land in 2005.* Page 3: *A home in Empire, LA, blocks 2 lanes of traffic.*
Page 4: *Aerial view of the Mississippi Gulf Coast damaged by Hurricane Katrina.* Back Cover: *Vessels block a highway after Katrina.*

Printed in China

HURRICANES

Stephen P. Leatherman
Jack Williams

Voyageur Press

Contents

Earth's Fiercest Storms

A hurricane's immense power – capable of killing thousands of people – captures the imagination of people around the world, even those who expect never to experience such a storm.

The complex interplay of forces that create hurricanes and similar storms makes them even more fascinating to those who want to learn a little about how nature works.

News images and reports of Hurricane Katrina's physical and human devastation to New Orleans and coastal areas of Louisiana, Mississippi, and Alabama, beginning on August 30, 2005, showed the world not only the power of a strong hurricane, but also the consequences both to individuals and to society of not being prepared to cope with such a storm despite ample warnings.

A couple of facts help illustrate the power of hurricanes:

- The average hurricane precipitates a trillion gallons of water a day.
- Hurricane Andrew had the equivalent power of an atomic bomb exploding every minute when it made landfall in South Florida in 1992.

Hurricanes are neither the largest nor strongest storms, but their combination of size and strength make them the deadliest and most destructive storms on Earth.

Big winter storms affect much larger areas and millions more people than even a storm like Katrina. A good example is the March 1993 'Storm of the Century,' which brought high winds and snow to the eastern United States from Alabama to New England, bringing traffic to a halt in cities from Birmingham, Alabama, to Boston, Massachusetts, and closing airports from Georgia to Maine. But the winds in such a

Photo by Astronaut Ed Lu from the International Space Station
shows Hurricane Isabel moving across the Atlantic Ocean toward North
Carolina with winds as fast as 120 mph, on September 15, 2003.

storm rarely blow faster than 74 mph hurricane force. (The term 'hurricane force' is often used to describe 74 mph or faster winds whether or not they are in a hurricane.) The strongest tornadoes, such as the one that flattened most of the small town of Greensburg, Kansas, on May 4, 2007 with winds faster than 200 mph, are more powerful than any hurricane. But a tornado that is a mile wide and lasts more than an hour is extremely large, long lasting, and rare.

Katrina is barely a hurricane as it hits Fort Lauderdale, Florida.

Tropical cyclones are one of the ways that nature keeps the Earth's heat budget in rough balance by moving warm air out of the tropics. Other kinds of storms also transport heat poleward as well as moving cold air toward the tropics. Ocean currents move warm water toward the poles and cold water toward the equator.

Hurricanes have existed since warm oceans first formed on Earth. People around the Pacific and Indian oceans as well as those in the Western Hemisphere before the arrival of Europeans knew about these storms and mostly learned how to live with them. In fact, hurricanes often bring welcome rain. Deadly Camille is an example of the bad and the good hurricanes can do. After hitting Mississippi in August 1969, Camille rapidly weakened and dropped approximately five inches of rain on parts of Kentucky and Tennessee, helping to ease a drought, before moving into the mountains of Virginia and West Virginia where it tapped into humid air from over the Atlantic Ocean to cause deadly floods.

The first Europeans on the record to encounter a hurricane were Christopher Columbus and his crews on their journeys to the New World. The word 'hurricane' came into English via the Spanish from the languages of the peoples who lived around the Caribbean Sea. Their storm god was called *hunraken*. In addition to learning a name for the fierce storms, which are unlike any that Europeans had ever encountered, the Spanish learned that hurricanes respect no one, including the Conquistadors who built a Spanish empire in the New World. Today's treasure hunters pluck gold coins and jewels from the bottom of the ocean in the Florida Keys and along the Atlantic Coast where hurricanes sunk Spanish treasure ships in the sixteenth, seventeenth, and eighteenth centuries.

Part of Slidell, Louisiana, a week after Hurricane Katrina hit in 2005.

Anyone today who lives on or visits a coast or an island that could be threatened by a hurricane, typhoon, or tropical cyclone would be wise to learn a few of the hard lessons these storms have been teaching from the time of Columbus through to May 2, 2008, when Cyclone Nargis hit Burma killing more than 100,000 people. This book's following chapters will help you begin this voyage of discovery.

Hurricane Basics

A satellite image of a mature hurricane offers the best way to begin understanding these violent storms. While the details of each hurricane are different, all of them have an eye at the storm's center, surrounded by bands of clouds. Winds in the eye, which can be from several miles to 100 miles across, are nearly calm; the storm's strongest winds are in the towering clouds circling the eye, known as the eye wall. Lines of clouds, called rain bands, which spiral in toward the eye wall, make up the rest of the hurricane that is visible from a satellite.

This storm organization means that as a hurricane hits land the winds grow stronger and stronger, then suddenly calm as the eye arrives. After a calm that can last a few minutes or more than an hour, winds suddenly start blowing as fast as they were just before the eye arrived, but from the opposite direction.

Warm, humid air from over the ocean fuels a hurricane. As the warm air rises into a hurricane's clouds it steadily grows colder, eventually reaching a temperature at which water vapor in the air (its humidity) begins condensing into the tiny water drops that make up a cloud. Cloud drops merge to form falling raindrops. When water vapor condenses, it releases the heat that originally went into evaporating water into air as vapor. This added heat offsets the cooling of the rising air to some extent, which means the air rises faster and farther that it would without the heat from condensing water vapor. Air from all around the hurricane flows into the storm to replace rising air, which creates the winds that spiral in toward the eye wall. The faster the air rises into the hurricane's clouds, the faster wind blows into the hurricane. Winds gain speed as they spiral toward the hurricane's center, reaching the fastest speeds in the eye wall. In the Northern Hemisphere the wind circles the

A NASA satellite image of Hurricane Isabel on September 15, 2003.

How Hurricanes Form

Solar radiation warms large areas of tropical oceans to 80° F (27°C) or hotter.

As warm, humid air rises, it cools.

Warm oceans set the stage for hurricanes

Warm ocean water evaporates, making the air for a few thousand feet above the ocean extremely humid.

Warm oceans and the warm, humid air above them are a potential source of energy for hurricanes.

Humidity in air begins condensing into cloud drops.

When humidity condenses it releases heat picked up when it evaporated. At times this provides energy for thunderstorms.

eye in a counterclockwise direction (looking down on the storm) while winds flow clockwise around similar Southern Hemisphere storms.

Since the speed of a hurricane's winds depends on how fast air is rising in the hurricane's thunderstorms, and since this speed depends on the temperature of the rising air, scientists call hurricanes 'heat engines.' Steam turbines that drive electric power generators and the engines in autos are other examples of heat engines, which convert heat into mechanical energy. A hurricane's winds do the work, as defined by physicists, of pushing up high waves and storm surge over the ocean, or topping trees and destroying buildings when a hurricane moves over land.

Ocean water needs to be approximately 80° Fahrenheit (26° Celsius) or warmer to supply the energy a hurricane needs to form, grow, and continue as a hurricane. In fact, if the layer of warm water is not at least 200 feet (60 meters) deep, the storm's wind can stir the ocean, bringing cold water to the top to weaken the hurricane. Since such warm oceans are found only in the tropics and subtropics, hurricanes and similar storms such as typhoons are called tropical cyclones. Other ingredients hurricanes need include a deep layer of humid air, and winds at all levels of the atmosphere that are blowing from generally the same direction at roughly the same speeds.

If these and other needed ingredients are in place, a disturbance in the northeasterly (from the northeast) trade winds can create a tropical depression, which is an area of clouds and rain with winds making a complete circle around a center. If the depression's fastest winds reach 39 mph (63 kph), it becomes a tropical storm and the National Hurricane Center gives it a name (See Chapter 4). When the winds reach 74 mph (119 kph), the storm becomes a hurricane.

A hurricane that moves over land or a cool ocean loses the ocean heat that powers it and thus begins dying. Sometimes a hurricane weakens when it is still over warm water because it moves into an area where high-altitude winds are blowing from

A three-dimensional, satellite view of Hurricane Linda on September 12, 1997 with winds estimated as 160 mph, making it the strongest known Eastern Pacific hurricane.

The 500 homes and other structures on Holly Beach, Louisiana were destroyed by Hurricane Rita's storm surge in 2005. The high surge, superimposed by hurricane-generated waves, carried the beach sand and debris far inland.

a different direction or faster than winds directly above the ocean's surface. When this happens, the opposing winds shear the storm apart and forecasters say that 'wind shear' has weakened it.

When a hurricane is over the ocean its wind energy begins to create the storm surge that can cause much of the damage when the storm hits land. While a hurricane's winds create both storm surge and huge waves, the two are different. A strong hurricane can whip up 50-foot (15-meter) or higher waves. While such waves can sink ships, they break down in shallow water when approaching land. In addition to creating waves, the wind circling a hurricane's eye in a tight spiral piles up water on the right side of the eye wall. The resulting mound of water moves ashore as a storm surge when the hurricane hits land. The hurricane's big waves ride ashore on top of the surge, significantly adding to the damage. Surge is sometimes described as a 'wall of water,' but it really arrives like a very quickly rising tide. Storm surge height depends on the hurricane's size and wind speed, depth and shape of the ocean bottom off shore, and other factors. Surge will be highest where it funnels into bays.

The effects of storm surge are somewhat like those of a tsunami, but the causes are completely different. Earthquakes or massive underwater landslides that disrupt the ocean's bottom cause tsunamis while the wind causes storm surge.

Almost all hurricanes occur during a hurricane season. This is because the water of large parts of the tropical Atlantic Ocean, the Caribbean Sea, and the Gulf of Mexico (collectively called the Atlantic Basin) are, on average, only warm enough for hurricanes during the June 1 through November 30 hurricane season. The most active part of the season runs from mid August through mid October when the water is warmest. From time to time, however, a hurricane will form outside the June-November season, possibly in early December or late May.

Once a tropical depression forms over the Atlantic Ocean it moves toward the west, pushed by the steady winds from just above the ocean to high in the atmosphere. A large area of high atmospheric pressure that can stretch halfway across the Atlantic, known as the Bermuda High, helps determine the day-to-day wind patterns that steer hurricanes. As with any area of high pressure at the Earth's surface, air sinks from the upper atmosphere and flows out over the ocean (or land) in a clockwise direction around the high-pressure area in the Northern Hemisphere (counterclockwise in the Southern Hemisphere). The generally east-to-west winds on the southern side of the Bermuda High steer hurricanes across the Atlantic toward the west. At times, the western end of the Bermuda High is over the ocean far from the U.S. East Coast. In this case, the clockwise winds steer hurricanes toward the northeast before the storms reach the United States. At other times the western end of the Bermuda High is farther west and its winds steer hurricanes across Florida, Cuba, or the Caribbean Sea, it may also turn storms toward the north into the Gulf of Mexico.

Weather systems other than the Bermuda High also affect hurricane paths. For example, a huge mass of cool, dry air moving toward the southeast from Canada into the eastern United States will push a hurricane away from the United States if the boundary between the cool air and the warmer air – called a cold front – reaches the hurricane when the storm is still far out over the ocean. But, if a similar cold front arrives after a storm has almost reached the East Coast, it can turn the hurricane to the north and then the northeast, possibly to hit North Carolina or states farther north.

As we will see in Chapter 4, in order to predict where a hurricane will hit, meteorologists have to forecast how the large-scale weather patterns such as the Bermuda High and cold fronts will change over the next few days.

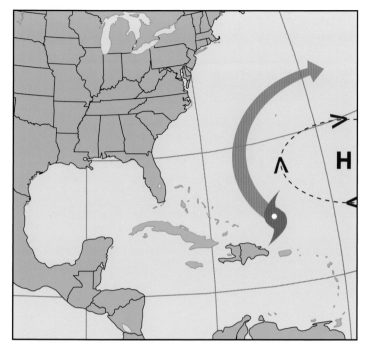

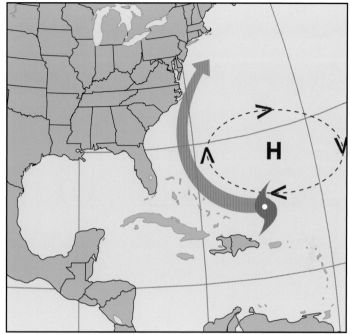

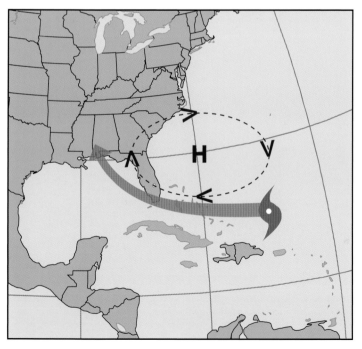

The Bermuda High Pressure System plays a major role in guiding hurricanes in the Atlantic Ocean. In 2004 and 2005, the Bermuda High was close to the U.S. East Coast, driving the hurricanes into Florida and the Gulf of Mexico. When the high moves further offshore, it opens up the corridor for hurricanes to move northward toward Cape Hatteras and Long Island. In 2006, the Bermuda High moved far eastward in the Atlantic Ocean, turning the tropical systems 270 degrees toward Europe and keeping them far away from the United States.

Unlocking Hurricane Mysteries

William C. Redfield, a businessman and self-taught scientist from Connecticut, is the father of hurricane science. In 1831 he published a study based on extensive examination of storm reports to show that a hurricane that hit the United States in 1821 consisted of winds blowing counterclockwise around a center. While wind speeds changed, they held the 'whirlwind' pattern as the storm moved in from the Atlantic Ocean, hit Virginia, moved up the coast, came ashore again over New York City, and then crossed New England. Until then even scientists did not know that all storms consist of a low-pressure center surrounded by winds.

Having a mental image of storm structure is only a first step toward forecasting. Telegraph lines that began linking large areas of Europe and the United States in the 1840s enabled meteorologists to begin predicting the weather. Using telegraphed reports, they drew weather maps showing weather patterns and applied what little they knew about meteorology to predict how the patterns would change over the next day or two.

While successful forecasts were sometimes made for winter storms, hurricanes were another matter. They come from the sea to hit the Bahamas, the islands around the Caribbean Sea, the United States, and Mexico. With no reports from over the oceans, meteorologists rarely managed to forecast when and where a hurricane would hit.

The first half of the 20th century saw some improvements in hurricane forecasting, but major hurricanes continued to hit with no warning. Noteworthy examples are the hurricane that smashed into the Florida Keys on Labor Day (September 2) 1935, killing more than 400 people. This was the strongest hurricane on record to hit the United States. On September 21, 1938 a hurricane hit Long

Hurricane Katrina's storm surge leaves boats on a highway in southern Louisiana.

Island, New York, and New England with winds faster than 100 miles an hour with absolutely no warning, killing more than 600 people.

The turning point came after World War II, thanks in part to technologies developed during the war. Radar was developed to detect enemy airplanes or ships hidden by fog, clouds, or distance. Radar sends out radio waves that reflect back from airplanes or ships. Scientists working on radar during World War II learned that raindrops, snowflakes, hail, sleet, and even cloud drops reflect radio waves, which interfered with spotting enemy airplanes and ships. They also realized that radar could also help detect dangerous weather such as thunderstorms, typhoons, and hurricanes.

The U.S. Highway 90 bridge between Pass Christian and Bay St. Louis, Mississippi, wrecked by Katrina.

During World War II radar also began teaching meteorologists things they had never before known about hurricanes. On September 14, 1944 the eye of the 'Great Atlantic Hurricane of 1944' passed by about sixty miles offshore from the Lakehurst (New Jersey) Naval Air Station. The station's radar showed the hurricane's structure with an eye wall and rain bands. This first view of a hurricane's structure, which until then had gone unrecognized, was one of the keys to a much better scientific understanding of hurricanes.

The radio waves used for radar do not follow the Earth's curvature, which means that by the time a hurricane shows up on land-based radar, it's almost always less than a day away from hitting. Radar does not work for warnings, but satellites were the answer. After World War II both the United States and the Soviet Union used captured German V-2 rockets as the basis of their space programs, which led to, among many other things, the launch of the first successful weather satellite on October 4, 1957, the U.S. *Tiros 1*. Only five days after launch it photographed a tropical cyclone over the Pacific Ocean 800 miles east of Brisbane, Australia, which no one had previously known about.

Advances after *Tiros 1* have given forecasters many new tools. One of the most important of these came in November 1960 with the launch of the *Tiros 2* satellite, which was equipped with a sensor that captured infrared (heat energy) images as well as the visual images that *Tiros 1* sent back. In addition to helping track storms at night, they indicate the temperatures of cloud tops. The colder the cloud tops, the higher they are, and cloud height depends on a storm's strength. (The tops of strong thunderstorms can be as high as 65,000 feet, which is twice as high as the cruising altitude of jet airliners.) As infrared imagers were developed over the years, they began showing water vapor (otherwise invisible) in the air, which helps forecasters track upper altitude winds, and see whether dry air that would weaken a hurricane is flowing into it.

The second big advance was the launch of the first Geostationary Operational (as opposed to research) Environmental Satellite (GOES) in 1975. Geostationary satellites orbit 22,238 miles (35,781 kilometers) above the equator at the same speed as Earth's rotation, which keeps them above the same spot on Earth, with storms in constant view. A constant view of a hurricane does not by itself tell forecasters where it's going to go. Data on patterns of air pressure and winds at all levels of the atmosphere help forecasters, but they also need to know how hurricanes work.

That knowledge grew slowly from the 19th century until the 1950s when six hurricanes hit the U.S. East Coast from North Carolina to New England in 1954 and 1955, causing billions of dollars in damage in a part of the country that had seen few hurricanes. The public outcry to 'do something about hurricanes' led the U.S. Congress to fund the National Hurricane Research Project, which began in 1956. Using the best technology of the time and military airplanes, scientists made flights into five hurricanes at various levels in 1957 and 1958, taking measurements that answered many questions, but raised many more. The project was the forerunner of the U.S. National Oceanic and Atmospheric Administration (NOAA) Hurricane Research Division in Miami, which continues learning about hurricanes.

One outgrowth of the Hurricane Research Project was Project Stormfury, which tried several times between 1962 and 1983 to weaken hurricanes by seeding them with silver iodide. There is evidence that such seeding can increase the amount of rain or snow that fall from clouds. The Stormfury idea was to seed a hurricane's outer rain bands, which could make them grow at the expense of the eye wall; thus weakening the storm. This seemed to work in a couple of cases, but scientists later learned that hurricanes naturally go through cycles of growing weaker and stronger, as had happened in the seeded storms.

Stormfury scientists also looked into other ideas, such as spreading something on the ocean surface that would inhibit evaporation, thus reducing a storm's fuel supply, and found none of the ideas worth pursuing. Writing for the 'frequently asked questions' section about hurricanes on NOAA's website, Chris Landsea, a hurricane researcher, summed up the weaknesses of suggestions for controlling hurricanes: 'They fail to appreciate the size and power of tropical cyclones… Perhaps if the time comes when men and women can travel at nearly the speed of light to the stars, we will then have enough energy for brute-force intervention in hurricane dynamics.'

Hurricane Hunters and Storm Chasers

The men and women who fly into hurricanes are used to being asked two questions: Don't you have to be crazy to fly into a hurricane? Do you fly over the top of the storm or around it? The answer to the first question is: The people who fly into hurricanes are not daredevils looking for a thrill, but professionals who know what they are doing. The answer to the second is: Almost all hurricane flights are right though the heart of the storm.

Since airplanes began flying into tropical cyclones in 1943, only four out of a few thousand missions have gone down in a storm: three in Pacific Ocean typhoons in 1951, 1958, and 1964, and one in a Caribbean Sea hurricane in 1955. All thirty-six men aboard the four airplanes were killed. The safety record is a testimony to the professionalism of those making the flights.

A NOAA P-3 pilot's view of Katrina's eye wall from inside the eye, on August 28, 2005, the day before the hurricane hit.

Airplanes are flown into hurricanes to provide the reliable and detailed wind data U.S. forecasters need to issue warnings for the many vulnerable areas along the coasts. Hurricane flights ensure the best possible forecasts and warnings, and the flights cost much less than the money they save. Flights are also essential for researchers who are improving forecasts by learning more about how these storms work. While forecasters use satellite images to estimate winds speeds, these are not as accurate as airplane measurements.

The WC-130 airplanes flown by the U.S. Air Force Reserve 53rd Weather Reconnaissance Squadron based in Biloxi, Mississippi, and the NOAA WP-3 airplanes, based in Tampa, Florida, fly through storms, usually 5,000 to 10,000 feet above the ocean. On a typical nine- or ten-hour flight, an airplane will make maybe a half dozen trips all of the way across a storm, following a different path each time. Each trip goes through the turbulent eye wall and the calm eye. The airplanes have weather radars, which help the pilots avoid the most turbulent parts of the storm while providing added storm data. The airplane's flight-management computers produce continuous readouts of the wind's speed and direction at the airplane's altitude. Meteorologists use these to estimate winds near the surface.

To collect even better, low-altitude data, the airplanes drop GPS dropsondes. These are 16-inch (40.6 cm) long, 2.75 in (6.98 cm) diameter tubes with sensors that measure temperature, air pressure, humidity, wind speed and direction, and radio those data to the airplane as they fall to the ocean, slowed by a small parachute. While dropsondes give precise wind data, it's for only a few locations in a storm. In 2005 the two NOAA WP-3s began using a device called a Stepped Frequency Microwave Radiometer (SFMR), and the devices were installed on the Air Force Reserve WC-130s for the 2007 season. These record the surface wind speeds throughout a storm as they fly back and forth in it. Knowing the distribution of winds throughout a storm enables forecasters to make better predictions of the winds and storm surge likely to hit all areas affected by a hurricane when it comes ashore.

Neither the WC-130s nor the WP-3s can fly high enough to go over the top of a hurricane, which can be more than 40,000 feet above the ocean. NOAA has one airplane, a Gulfstream IV jet, which can fly as high as 45,000 feet, but its main mission is to fly high over large areas of ocean around a hurricane, measuring the winds that are steering the storm. NASA's ER-2, a civilian version of the U-2 spy plane, has flown as high as 60,000 feet above hurricanes collecting data. Perhaps more important for forecasters is the data collected by flying low into a hurricane, which can really only be accomplished by drones. These small, pilotless planes can sample close to the ocean's surface, and retrieve valuable information.

Researchers and forecasters are also working to collect better data about the winds after a storm comes ashore. A Doppler weather radar unit mounted on a flatbed truck – The Doppler on Wheels (DOW) – which University of Oklahoma scientists developed for tornado research, began unlocking some of the mysteries of hurricane winds above land the evening of September 6, 1996 when Hurricane Fran came ashore near Wilmington, North Carolina. The DOW, parked at the Wilmington International Airport, discovered a hurricane feature scientists didn't yet known about: 'wind rolls.' This refers to a rolling wind pattern that brings down high-speed wind to smash into the ground. Such wind rolls could have caused the narrow streaks of incredible damage that Hurricane Andrew left when it hit Miami, Florida, in 1992. The DOWs are continuing to fill in gaps in hurricane wind knowledge.

The damaging U.S. hurricanes of 2004 and 2005 rekindled a debate about the actual speeds of hurricane winds near the ground. Such information is critical for relating peak speeds to observed damage. In addition, while ordinary wind measurements are of 'sustained' winds – an average over a short period of time – scientists and engineers need data on gust speeds to determine the actual wind loads on structures, which are needed to modify building codes.

The Florida Coastal Monitoring Program is a joint venture of Clemson University, University of Florida, and Florida International University that focuses on full-scale measurement of near-surface hurricane winds and the resultant loads on residential structures. The goal is to provide data necessary to identify methods to cost-effectively reduce hurricane wind damage. The program uses a set of four portable towers to measure the time history of wind velocity at 5- and 10-meter (16- and 33-foot) heights. These meteorological towers, which also include measurements of barometric pressure, rainfall, temperature, and relative humidity, can be rapidly deployed into the path of an oncoming hurricane and will presumably survive 200-mph (322 kph) winds, though this has not yet been tested to date.

Before Hurricane Katrina hit in 2005, one tower was set up just south of New Orleans. After the full devastation caused by Katrina was discovered, the media reported that category 4 Katrina had wreaked havoc on New Orleans, including serious damage to the Superbowl and the downtown high-rise Hyatt Regency Hotel, which had its windows blown out, not to mention the breeching of the levees and flooding of 80 percent of New Orleans. The meteorological tower showed otherwise: New Orleans experienced 85 mph (137 kph), category 1 winds. The wind damage was the result more of inferior building codes and construction than wind speeds. Inadequate construction and maintenance, not overtopping by the storm surge, also caused the critical levee failure along Lake Pontchartrain.

In another effort to collect detailed landfall data, the International Hurricane Research Center is deploying fifty water-level gauges before hurricane landfall to quantify storm surge levels. These gauges will enable researchers to determine the amount of damage from wind vs. surge, which is of primary interest to insurance companies, because many policies pay for wind damage, but not flood damage. They will also provide valuable calibration and verification of surge-prediction models.

A close up view of Hurricane Isabel's eye over the Atlantic on September 13, 2003.

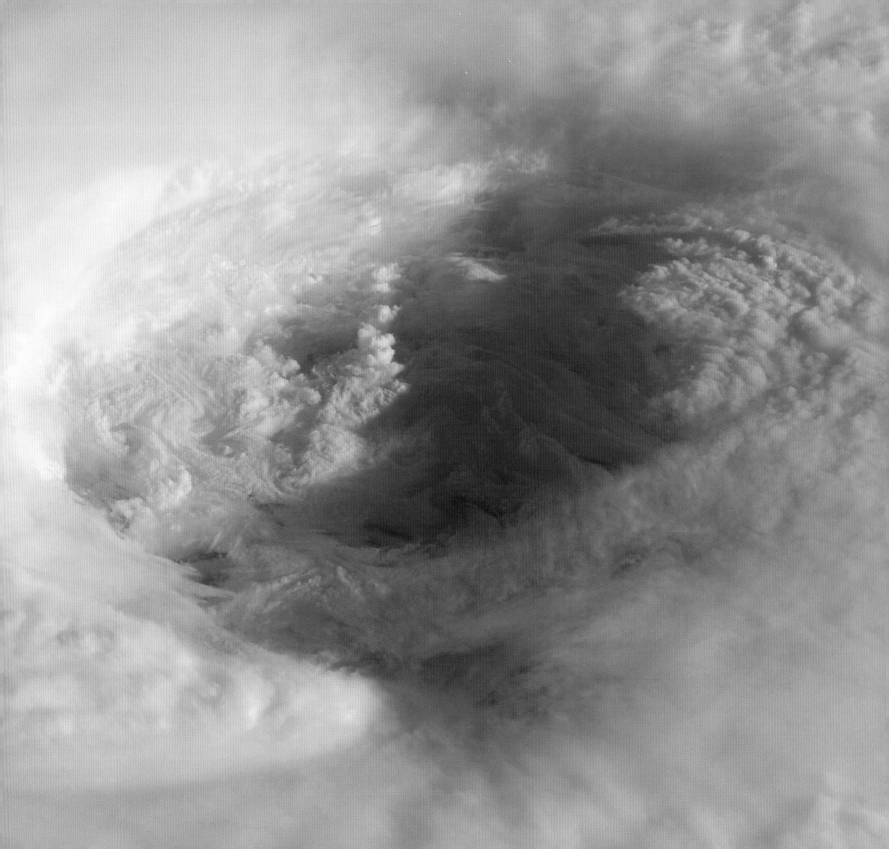

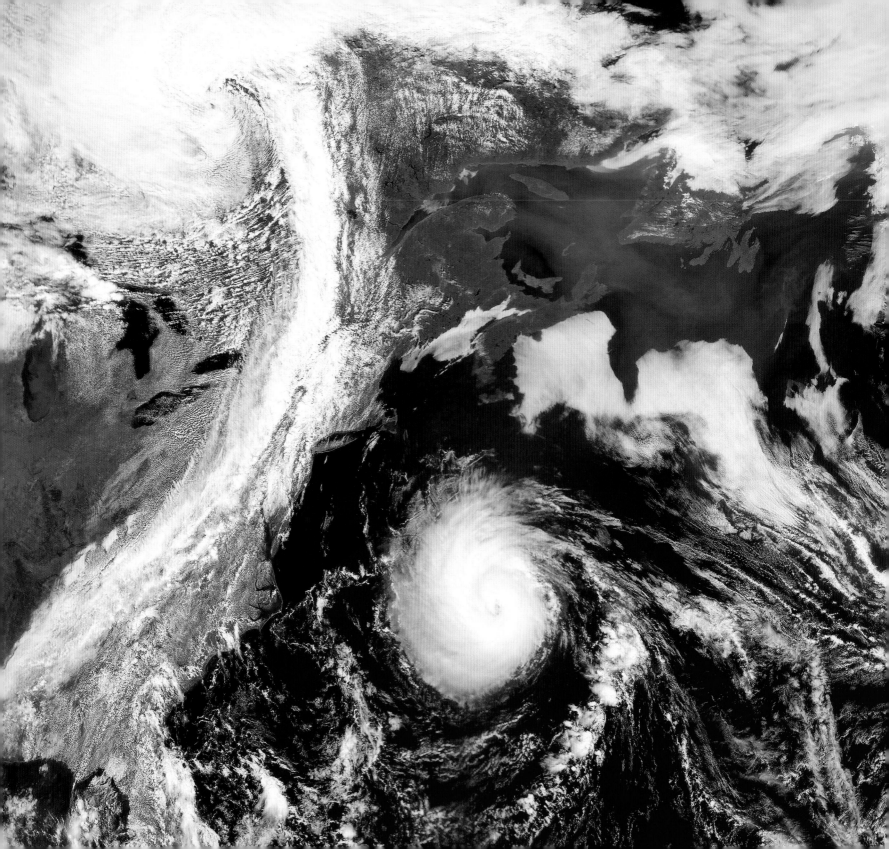

Hurricane Forecasting

When a hurricane threatens the United States, Mexico, Central America or the islands around the Caribbean Sea, people who might be affected turn to the National Hurricane Center (NHC) for authoritative forecasts.

As part of the U.S. National Weather Service (NWS), the NHC on the Florida International University campus west of downtown Miami, produces tropical storm and hurricane forecasts for the Atlantic Basin and the eastern Pacific Ocean west to the 140 degrees longitude line. The NHC is the World Meteorological Organization's (WMO) center responsible for all tropical cyclone forecasts in these areas, which means that NHC forecasters work with meteorologists from other nations affected by hurricanes, such as Mexico, The Bahamas, and the various Caribbean islands. The center issues tropical storm and hurricane watches and warnings for the United States after talking with NWS offices and emergency management officials in areas likely to be affected. The NHC recommends the timing and coverage of watches and warnings for other nations, after consulting with meteorologists in nations in the storm's path, but each nation's weather service issues the watches and warnings.

A hurricane watch means that hurricane-force winds are possible within thirty-six hours. A hurricane warning means that such winds are expected within twenty-four hours. Deciding what areas watches and warnings should cover and when they should be issued requires predicting where the hurricane will go and how strong it will be at various times in the future.

Making such predictions, as with any weather forecast, begins with collecting as much data as possible about what the weather is doing at the current time. Weather

A cold front, which is marked by clouds along the U.S. East Coast, is moving toward the east to push Hurricane Erin away from North America on September 10, 2001.

stations, weather balloons, weather radars, aircraft, and satellites collect temperatures, humidity levels, air pressures, and wind speeds and directions both at the surface and aloft from around the globe. Much of this information is fed into supercomputers that use programs, called models, which are based on the physical laws that govern the atmosphere. The computer models produce forecasts for periods ranging from an hour in the future to days or even weeks ahead. Some of the forecasts are general outlines of global weather patterns while others focus on more detailed predictions such as for a particular hurricane.

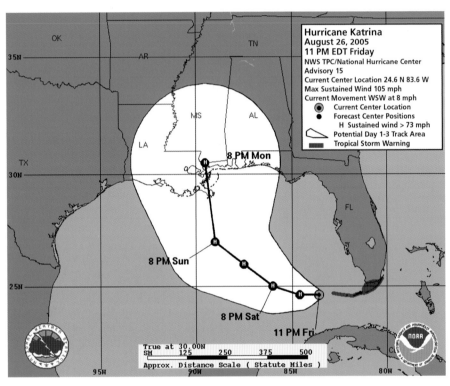

Hurricane Katrina
August 26, 2005
11 PM EDT Friday
NWS TPC/National Hurricane Center
Advisory 15
Current Center Location 24.6 N 83.6 W
Max Sustained Wind 105 mph
Current Movement WSW at 8 mph
⊙ Current Center Location
● Forecast Center Positions
H Sustained wind > 73 mph
Potential Day 1-3 Track Area
Tropical Storm Warning

True at 30.00N
SM   125   250   375   500
Approx. Distance Scale (Statute Miles)

Katrina's forecast and cone of uncertainty before it hit land.

The NHC's hurricane forecasters, with assistance from other Center specialists, issue forecasts every six hours regarding a hurricane's track and intensity for the next 12, 24, 36, 48, 72, 96 and 120 hours. To do this, the specialists use the output from the different models and their expert knowledge of hurricanes, the weather systems that affect them, and of the strengths and shortcomings of each model. The NHC communicates these forecasts via text bulletins designed for not only the general public, but also for other meteorologists and for particular groups such as captains of any ships near a storm. The NHC also produces maps and other graphics, including a table showing the probabilities of various wind speeds at different times in the future.

The most familiar map has dots for each forecast location out to five days ahead and a line connecting the dots showing the storm's predicted path. These NHC maps also include a 'forcast cone of uncertainty' a circular area which represents the probable track of the hurricane, but accounts for the fact that forecasters cannot predict exactly where a storm will go, and the further in the future the forecast is, the more unlikely it is to be accurate. Everyone threatened by a hurricane should understand:

- A hurricane is not a point like those on forecast maps. Its winds and surge could affect more than 200 miles of coastline.

- The forecast cone is based on the eye's forecast positions, not a hurricane's size or wind speeds; hurricane-force winds and surge could extend well outside the cone.

- The average forecast error for each time period over the previous ten years is used to construct the cone.

- The eye can be expected to move outside the cone approximately one third of the time.

The bottom line is the that forecast cone is not a guarantee of where a hurricane's eye will go, much less where its wind and surge will be felt. Don't bet your life on the forecast track of a hurricane.

The NHC makes all of its forecasts and maps available on its website as soon as they are issued, but most people rely on the news media for the latest information. When a strong hurricane appears to threaten the United States, broadcast and print journalists scramble to send the latest news to the public. Telephone calls from journalists around the world flood the Center during dangerous hurricanes.

The U.S. television networks (broadcasting in both English and Spanish) and local stations in threatened areas broadcast regular interviews from the NHC with the director, or other forecasters. Some networks and stations create their own forecast

maps based on the NHC forecasts and the opinions of their own meteorologists. While some of their maps might differ slightly from NHC maps, the points above still apply.

When the NHC specialists decide that a tropical storm has formed, they give it the next name on that year's pre-approved list. Since the 1979 season, men's and women's names in English, French, and Spanish have been used. They are on six lists adopted by the WMO's Western Hemisphere Hurricane Committee. Each list is used for one year's storms and then used again six years later with an important exception: the names of especially deadly or destructive hurricanes are retired and replaced by the Hurricane Committee at its meeting the following spring.

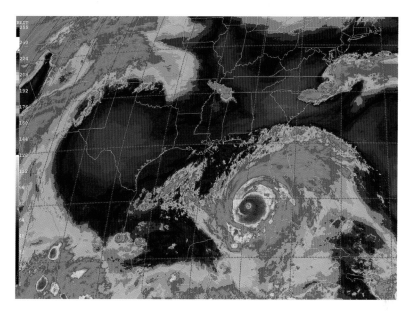

Water vapor satellite image of Hurricane Rita.

When a storm becomes a hurricane the NHC begins listing its category on the Saffir-Simpson damage potential scale. Herbert Saffir, a consulting engineer and a wind damage authority in Coral Gables, Florida, developed the scale for wind damage in the 1960s. Robert Simpson, who was director of the National Hurricane Center from 1967 through 1973, correlated the wind speeds with potential storm surge for the scale that the NHC has used in its public advisories since 1975.

View from the International Space Station clearly shows rain bands spiraling into Hurricane Claudette over the Gulf of Mexico on July 15, 2003.

The categories are only a very general guide to the damage expected from a storm because surges can be much higher or much lower depending upon the hurricane size and characteristics of the landfall area. Also, the categories give no hint about how extensive or deep the fresh-water floods caused by a hurricane's rain will be.

THE SAFFIR-SIMPSON DAMAGE POTENTIAL SCALE			
CATEGORY	WINDS	STORM SURGE	
1	74-95 mph (119-153 kph)	4-5 feet (1.2-1.5 m)	Little damage to building structures. Most damage to unanchored mobile homes, shrubbery, and trees.
2	96-110 mph (154-177 kph)	6-8 feet (1.8-2.4 m)	Limited damage to roofs, windows, and doors. Some trees blown down. Considerable damage to mobile homes. Flooding of coastal roads and escape routes 2-4 hours before the hurricane arrives.
3	111-130 mph (178-209 kph)	9-12 feet (2.7-3.7 m)	Some structural damage to small houses. Foliage blown off trees and large trees blown down. Mobile homes destroyed. Rising water cuts low-lying escape routes 3-5 hours before the storm arrives.
4	131-155 mph (210-149 kph)	13-18 feet (4-5 m)	Some complete roof failure on small houses. Shrubs, trees, and all signs blown down. Complete destruction of mobile homes. Extensive damage to doors and windows. Low-lying escape roads flooded 3-5 hours before arrival of the hurricane.
5	Greater than 155 mph (249 kph)	More than 18 feet (5 m)	Complete roof failure of houses and industrial buildings. Some complete building failure. Major damage to lower floors of all buildings less than 15 feet above sea level.

The most important rule for staying safe in a hurricane is to evacuate or ensure you are in a building that's well above the highest-possible surge level and sturdy enough to stand up to the highest likely wind if you are in an area for which a warning is posted. This applies even though a forecast map seems to show the hurricane will hit more than 100 miles away.

Hurricane Fran moving toward the northwest past the Bahamas on its way to hit North Carolina in September 1996.

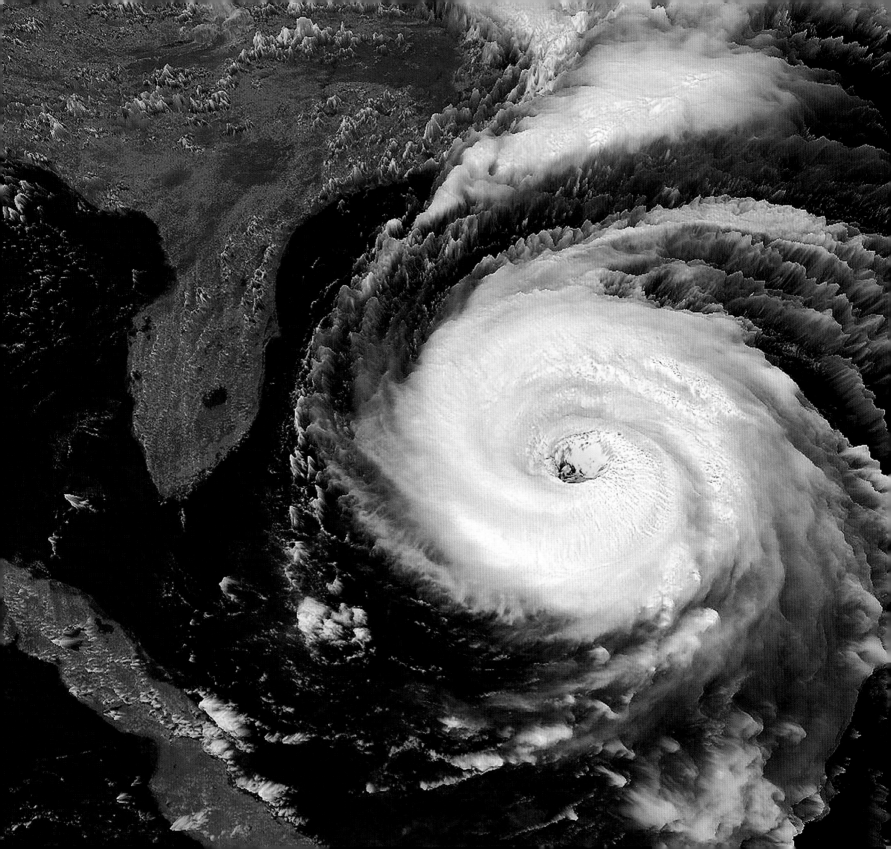

Living With Hurricanes

Hurricane winds receive most of the news media attention, but they are merely the beginning of the dangers. In addition to wind damage, a hurricane's hazards include storm surge, freshwater flooding, beach erosion, and rip currents.

The two worst places to be during a hurricane are in a coastal area where storm surge could flood your living room, or if you are stuck in a traffic jam where wind-borne debris could crash through your car windows.

If you are among the thousands of people who have recently moved to a coastal area or among the thousands more who vacation in places hurricanes can hit, the best quick summary of what to do when a hurricane is heading your way is:

• Run from the water.

• Hide from the wind.

While hurricanes regularly hit the U.S. East and Gulf Coasts, fortunately they are rare for any particular location, even those with the highest odds of being hit such as southern Florida or North Carolina's Outer Banks. Since it's impossible to say more than a few days ahead of time where a hurricane is going to hit, anyone who lives in the potential danger zone needs a hurricane plan.

The 'run from water' rule means you should learn whether a storm surge could flood your home. If so, a hurricane watch for your area means you should evacuate early to avoid getting stuck in a traffic jam.

U.S. Census data shows that more than 11 million people live in places where a storm surge could flood. One way to learn in advance whether your home is in a potential surge zone is to check with your county or municipal emergency management

Large parts of New Orleans remain flooded two weeks after Hurricane Katrina's storm surge overwhelmed several levees.

office. Maps of potential surge areas have been prepared for all areas along the U.S. Atlantic and Gulf coasts, and also for Puerto Rico. Unfortunately, few people take the time to learn about the surge danger before a hurricane threatens them. Then, many cannot relate two-dimensional maps of evacuation zones to their three-dimensional experiences. To address this problem, the International Hurricane Research Center in Miami, Florida, is developing real-time, 3-D computer animations of storm surge zones that could be shown on television.

The 'hide from the wind' rule means that if your home is away from a surge zone, is well built, and the windows and sliding glass doors are either made of impact-resistant glass or protected by shutters, you are probably safest sheltering at home, if you have the needed supplies.

If you live in a mobile or manufactured home or in a house you don't trust to protect you from wind, you should flee. You are not necessarily safe in a high-rise building. Winds at the level of higher floors are stronger than at ground level; they could blow out windows or even rip away outer walls. Even if the building isn't damaged, you could face days without electricity, which means no air conditioning or elevator service, and possibly no water.

Ensuring your home will be a safe hurricane shelter begins when you build or buy it. Most people buy homes based on the number of bedrooms and bathrooms, or the location without thinking about how storm-worthy the house might be. A homebuyer who wants a house that will survive a hurricane might not know what to look for. Even if the house meets the requirements of the local building code, a buyer can't be sure it would survive a hurricane.

Researchers at the International Hurricane Research Center (IHRC) in Miami, Florida, hope its new 'Wall of Wind' testing facility will have the effects similar to the well-publicized crash tests of cars. The crash tests made buyers more safety conscious

Storm Surges

❶ Wind spiraling toward the storm's center piles up a mound of water that can be more than 50 miles across on the right, front side of the eye. The clockwise winds of Southern Hemisphere cyclones create a mound of water on the left, front side of the eye.

❸ Water rising into the low atmospheric pressure at the storm's center can slightly increase the height of the mound of water.

As a hurricane or other tropical cyclone comes ashore it brings a mound of water ashore called storm surge. A strong hurricane or cyclone moving across shallow ocean water offshore, such as in the *Gulf of Mexico* or the *Bay of Bengal* off Bangladesh, causes the largest storm surge.

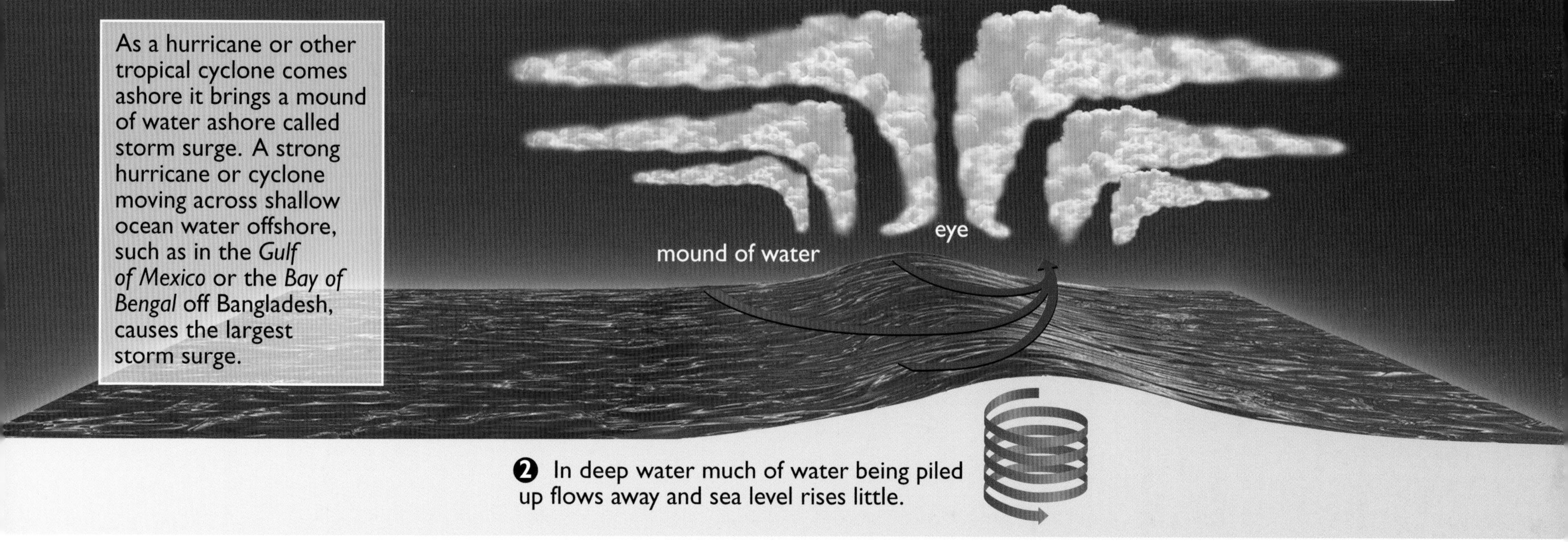

mound of water

eye

❷ In deep water much of water being piled up flows away and sea level rises little.

Since the combination of astronomical tide and surge determines the amount of flooding when a hurricane moves ashore, the most-dangerous storms are those that hit land at high tide.

A high tide that's 3 feet above mean sea level combined with a 12-foot storm surge would bring water 15 feet higher than mean sea level.

The same surge with a low tide, 3 feet below mean sea level would bring 9 feet of water.

Storm surge comes ashore like a rapidly rising tide, not like a "wall of water." In addition to the surge's flooding, waves on top of the surge batters structures nearest to the ocean.

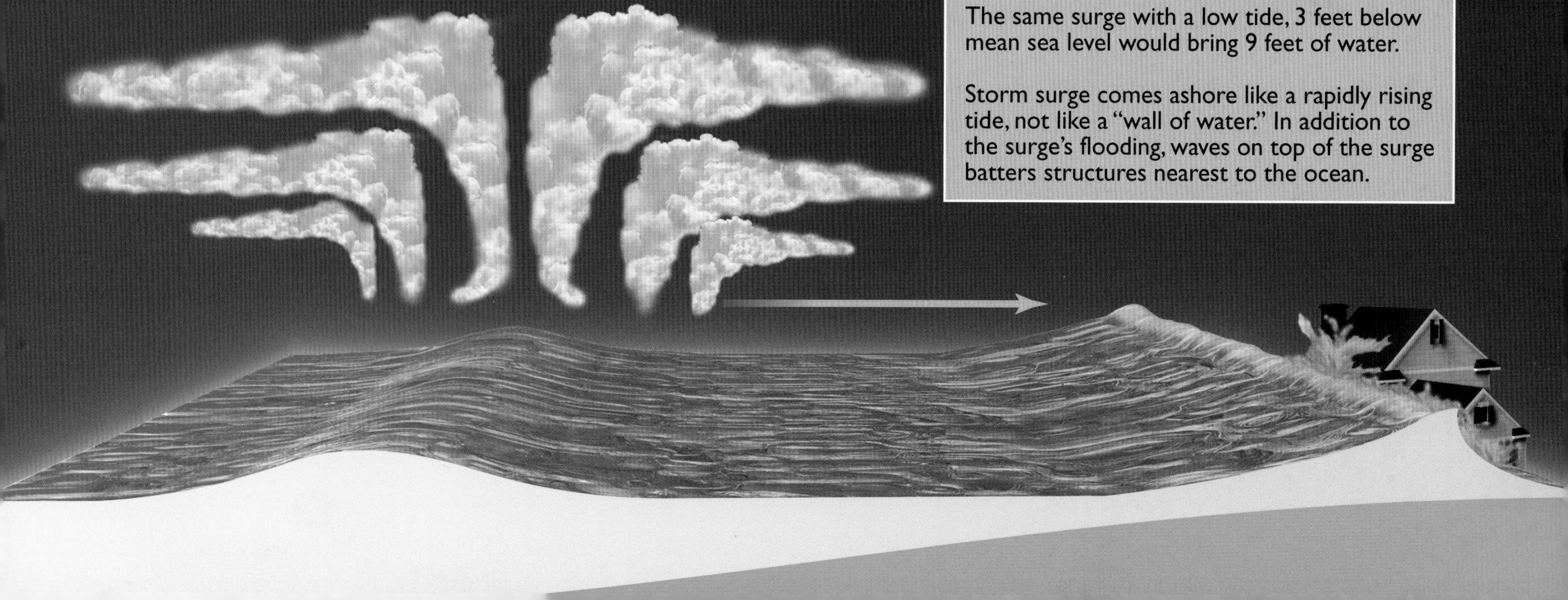

and helped engineers design safer vehicles. The researchers expect that television images of hurricane simulator experiments will drive home what a hurricane can do to a house while helping scientists and engineers develop better building standards.

Unlike previous wind tunnel testing of models of houses, the Wall of Wind uses large fans to blow hurricane-force winds against real buildings. A vacant house, which was scheduled for demolition, was hit with 120 mph (193 kph) winds and water to simulate rain by a 2-fan prototype in 2006. The 10-minute test left the home a total loss with the front door broken in, roof shingles peeling off, and windows shattered. The simulated wind-driven rain saturated the inside of the house; water seeped inside the walls, bubbling the paint and showing the potential for mold infestation. Huge pieces of the water-saturated ceiling tiles fell to the floor, and joints of the roof trusses were knocked askew. In its next phase, IHRC researchers are now using the 'RenaissanceRe' 6-fan Wall of Wind — capable of generating cat 4 winds, and a larger hurricane simulation is presently under development.

Even after a hurricane comes ashore and its winds weaken, it can be very dangerous. Between 1970 and 2004 'freshwater' flooding from rain caused 71 percent of U.S hurricane and tropical storm deaths, with many of these occurring far inland.

Tropical Storm Allison in 2001 illustrates how dangerous a storm even without a hurricane's 74 mph or stronger winds can be. Allison dropped more than 40 inches of rain on Texas. The worst flooding occurred in downtown Houston where over 2700 homes were destroyed and 30,000 people became homeless. Allison killed 41 people. There were ghastly stories of drownings when elevator doors opened into a flooded lobby area.

While tourists who only visit hurricane zones do not have to worry about losing their home to a storm, they should be aware of potential dangers when thinking of traveling to ocean resorts in the tropics, or to U.S. East and Gulf Coast beaches.

Planning a Caribbean vacation during the June through November hurricane season makes sense because the rates are low, but it could lead to some unpleasant experiences, such as those of the estimated 40,000 tourists caught in Cancun, Mexico, as Hurricane Wilma heavily damaged the resort in October 2005. This hurricane inched across the region over three days, trapping tourists and residents in buildings without air conditioning, and with shortages of food and drink. Fortunately, no deaths were reported but thousands of tourists sweltered for days waiting for flights home.

Many resorts offer hurricane insurance, but you should be sure you understand what is and what is not covered. Cruise ship vacations to hurricane-prone areas can be more of an adventure than you counted on; even if the ship is not directly affected by the winds, the big waves can travel for hundreds and even thousands of miles, making people seasick.

Hurricane Georges' storm surge surprised Key West residents.

THE MOST VULNERABLE AREAS OF THE USA

New Orleans

A week after Hurricane Katrina devastated New Orleans in August 2005, a poll conducted for the Associated Press found that 54 percent of Americans favored abandoning the flooded parts of the city. They were echoing proposals by some disaster experts to relocate the port and most of the city's businesses and residents up the

Mississippi River, leaving historic areas such as the French Quarter as tourist attractions. Another course, which public officials from President George W. Bush down to the local level quickly endorsed, was to rebuild New Orleans. It could have been rebuilt as a model of natural hazard mitigation, including elevating structures, turning very low-lying devastated areas into parks and restored wetlands, enacting better building codes, and building stronger levees and flood walls to protect large areas of the city, which is mostly below sea level.

Neither is happening, as Joel K. Bourne, Jr. wrote in the August 2007 *National Geographic* magazine: 'Instead of rebuilding smarter or surrendering, New Orleans is doing what it has always done after such disasters: bumping up the levees just a little higher, rebuilding the same flood-prone houses back in the same low spots, and praying that hurricanes hit elsewhere.' Such thinking, which has a three-century history, is one reason why New Orleans remains the most vulnerable area in the United States for another hurricane disaster.

Lake Okeechobee, Florida

An estimated 2,500 people drowned during the Great Lake Okeechobee Flood of 1928 when the storm surge and breaking waves driven by a Category 4 hurricane breached the dike that contains this third-largest lake entirely within the United States. It can happen again.

Lake Okeechobee is a shallow bowl-shaped lake, 35 miles in length north to south and 30 miles east to west. The water is normally only eleven to eighteen feet deep. This makes the lake especially susceptible to exceptionally large storm surges because wind from a Category 4 hurricane would push water from all depths of the shallow lake; much like someone blowing hard on a small saucer filled with water.

The 140-mile long Herbert Hoover Dike is supposed to protect people who live

Coastal erosion is one of the major impacts from hurricanes along with wind damage, storm surge inundation, and freshwater flooding. Roads can be washed away where beaches and dunes are lacking or eroded. Houses built on sandy bluffs or dunes are extremely vulnerable to being undermined, and toppling to the surf below.

along the north and south shores of Lake Okeechobee. But, the U.S. Army Corps of Engineers built it with porous materials, which means high lake levels may allow water to seep through the dike, causing it to fail for the same reason the New Orleans levees failed. This time 40,000 people would be endangered.

The Florida Keys

The beautiful azure waters of the Florida Keys have long attracted residents and visitors, and the U.S. Census Bureau estimates that 75,000 people live on the islands with one-third of them in Key West, at the extreme tip of the chain. When a hurricane threatens, emergency managers would prefer to evacuate everyone because a storm surge could sweep entirely across the small islands with elevations averaging 5 to 10 feet above sea level. Yet, Keys tourists and residents have only one route out: a two-lane highway that crosses forty-two bridges in the 126 miles from Key West to the mainland.

Evacuation can be a major problem in densely populated coastal areas.

Many Key residents hunker down when government officials 'order' them to evacuate. They fear being caught in traffic and then hit by flying debris or swept off the road by storm surge during the more than twenty-four hours needed to get everyone to shelter on the mainland. Nearly 50 percent of the residents chose not to evacuate

Destruction in the Ninth Ward of New Orleans three weeks after Hurricane Katrina's flooding pushed as much as eight feet of water over the neighborhood.

for the Category 3 Hurricane Georges in 1998. Many were surprised that the relatively low 5-foot storm surge knocked some houses off of their foundations. Yet, Georges' strongest winds missed the Keys.

Miami-Ft. Lauderdale

In 1926 approximately 30,000 people lived in fast-growing Miami when a hurricane

Toppled power lines add to the problems of damaged areas.

(they didn't have names then) hit with 135 mph winds and twelve to fifteen feet of storm surge. The hurricane basically cleaned out the shoddy construction of that era in Miami and Miami Beach. The 1926 damage and the damage of other hurricanes that hit in the 1940s, 1950s, and 1960s encouraged South Florida officials to enact some of the country's most stringent building codes. From 1965 until 1992 when major hurricanes hit elsewhere and newcomers with no hurricane experience flooded into the region, these stringent building codes do not seem to have been upheld. In August 1992 Hurricane Andrew, missed the heart of Miami, but destroyed more than 25,000 homes and damaged another 101,000 structures in Miami-Dade County. It exposed many failures to enforce building codes and brutally illustrated ways in which the codes should be improved. The Miami-Ft. Lauderdale metro area, where more than six million people live in a twenty- to thirty-mile-wide

A shop in New Orleans is open in October 2005 as debris from hurricanes Katrina and Rita remains to be hauled away. Due to the extensive damage and loss of life caused by these two storms, their names have been retired from the WMO list of hurricane names.

The Great Hurricane of 1900 devastated Galveston, Texas, and killed more than 6,000 people.

corridor between the Atlantic Ocean and the Everglades, is the most hurricane-prone area in the United States. In addition to being packed with very expensive property along the Atlantic Ocean, the region has a large population of poorer people and retirees of modest means; people who are especially vulnerable to disasters. If a twin of the 1926 hurricane hit the area today – roaring across the center of Miami – it could be the most expensive disaster in U.S. history, topping $100 billion.

Galveston and Houston

Memories of the 1900 hurricane held back the development of Galveston, Texas, for the next six decades, while Houston, with the city's center fifty miles inland, was growing into the fourth-largest city in the United States. Since then, however, the population on Galveston Island has soared with homes and businesses spreading beyond the area protected by the seawall that was built after the Great 1900 Hurricane destroyed Galveston. A tropical storm in 2001 and a hurricane that missed in 2005 illustrate the vulnerabilities of this sprawling, flat area to many storm hazards. Tropical Storm Allison's winds never reached 74 mph hurricane speed, but it stalled over downtown Houston for several days, with its rain causing freshwater floods that drowned forty-one people and displaced more than 30,000 families. Allison's $5 billion in damage was the highest in Texas history.

In September 2005 when officials ordered an evacuation of Galveston Island and other areas that Hurricane Rita's surge could threaten, roughly half of the area's five million people – this was only three weeks after Katrina devastated New Orleans – headed north and west in their cars. Rita veered to the north, making landfall in western Louisiana, sparing the Galveston-Houston area from serious damage.

Ninety of the 111 Rita-related deaths in Texas occurred on the highways. These included twenty-three elderly men and women killed when the bus evacuating them from a nursing home caught fire. The 100-degree temperatures and lack of care for existing medical conditions killed many other evacuees. Many who fled lived outside possible surge zones and would have been safe from wind in well-built homes or local shelters. As Rita showed, some evacuations can be a disaster.

Hurricane Isabel's wind and storm surge batter the Outer Banks of North Carolina on September 18, 2003.

Outer Banks of North Carolina

Atlantic hurricanes that miss Florida by turning to the north and then the northeast often hit the string of narrow barrier islands off the North Carolina coast called the Outer Banks. Over the years, hurricanes have sent water completely across the islands and cut new inlets between the ocean and the sounds. The Cape Hatteras and Cape Lookout National Seashores have restricted development along more than 120 miles of the easternmost banks, but islands to the north and south are heavily developed.

Any weekend from June through September more than 120,000 people are likely to be in the Cape Hatteras National Seashore or the crowded resort towns, such as Nags Head to the north, with only two highway bridges as escape routes. The Outer Banks have the nation's third-highest odds of being hit by a hurricane during any one season, behind only the Miami-Fort Lauderdale area and the Upper Florida Keys.

*A week after Hurricane Katrina hit, flood water still surrounds
many homes and businesses in New Orleans.*

Long Island and New York City

While the odds of a hurricane, especially a major hurricane with 110 mph (177 kph) winds, hitting New York City are much lower than for most places along the U.S. East and Gulf of Mexico coasts, the potential consequences can be much greater. The worst scenario would be a strong hurricane that moved north along the New Jersey coast with its strongest right side over the ocean. The coasts of New Jersey and Long Island would funnel the surge from such a storm into New York Harbor to flood places such as John F. Kennedy Airport and the southern part of Manhattan. Water from such a surge would wash into the New York Subway system, causing tremendous damage and the possible loss of thousands of lives.

The greatest hurricane to strike the Northeast U.S. coast in the memory of people living today was the Great New England Hurricane of 1938. While most hurricanes move along their path with forward speeds of 12 mph, this hurricane sped northward at speeds greater than 50 mph, catching the forecasters and the public totally off-guard since no satellites or hurricane hunters tracked storms at that time.

This hurricane produced a large storm surge that overtopped much of the barrier islands from Fire Island to East Hampton, Long Island, destroying most all of the beachfront buildings and cutting scores of inlets through the barrier beaches. After crossing Long Island, the hurricane pushed a storm surge into Narragansett Bay that flooded buildings in downtown Providence, Rhode Island, to their second floors. About 700 people perished during this storm, mostly drowning in the salty waters of the surge. Since 1938 Long Island, New York, has grown to a population of six million.

Clouds starting at the top of the image trace cool, dry air spiraling into Isabel, weakening it, as the hurricane comes ashore in 2003.

Cyclones and Typhoons

While not nearly as many tropical cyclones occur in the Indian Ocean as in the Atlantic Basin, over the years tropical cyclones in the Bay of Bengal, which is the part of the Indian Ocean on the eastern side of India, have created the world's deadliest storm surges. Records going back to the sixteenth century show that Indian Ocean cyclones moving into the Bay have killed thousands of people when they flood low-lying coastal areas of what is now Bangladesh.

In fact, the tropical cyclone that hit this region in November 1970 when it was East Pakistan is probably the deadliest storm in world history. Estimates of the death toll range from 300,000 to 500,000. Dissatisfaction with Pakistan's central government's response to the disaster added to existing unrest in East Pakistan. This helped lead to the Bangladesh Liberation War in 1971, which made Bangladesh a separate nation.

After another cyclone in 1991 killed an estimated 60,000 people in Bangladesh, the nation improved its warning services with the help of the World Meteorological Organization, and built concrete shelters atop dirt mounds in the low-lying Ganges River Delta at the head of the Bay of Bengal. Since then the death tolls from cyclones have dropped. For instance a 1998 storm destroyed the homes of more than 80,000 people but killed fewer than 200.

Cyclones also form on the western side of India in the Arabian Sea, but rarely threaten land. Rarely does not mean never. For instance in June 2007 Cyclone Gonu reached an estimated wind speed of at least 131 mph (211 kph), prompting the evacuation of thousands of people in Oman and then Iran. Oman reported the storm killed 49 people but death figures from Iran were not made available.

An image of the Earth's full disc from the GOES 12 satellite shows the Category 5 Hurricane Dean coming ashore on Mexico's Yucatan Peninsula on August 20, 2007.

This map shows in red the 'basins' where most of the world's tropical cyclones form. The dashed lines show a few of the hundreds of paths tropical cyclones take after they form. 'Hurricanes,' 'typhoons', and 'cyclones' are the names for storms with winds 74 mph or faster in each region. Most tropical cyclones form in the tropics, the latitudes approximately 1,600 miles north or south of the equator. In this region, east to west winds generally push storms toward the west. Large areas of high atmospheric pressure such as the Bermuda high, dominate the latitudes just north and south of the tropics. Many tropical cyclones turn toward the poles (north in the Northern Hemisphere, south in the Southern Hemisphere) around the western ends of these high-pressure areas. The exact locations and strengths of these high-pressure areas are major factors determining where storms travel.

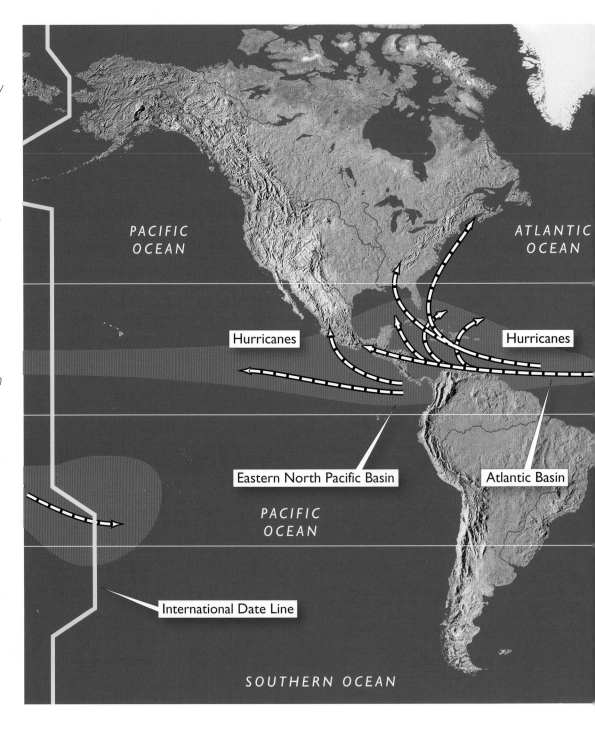

PACIFIC OCEAN

ATLANTIC OCEAN

Hurricanes

Hurricanes

Eastern North Pacific Basin

Atlantic Basin

PACIFIC OCEAN

International Date Line

SOUTHERN OCEAN

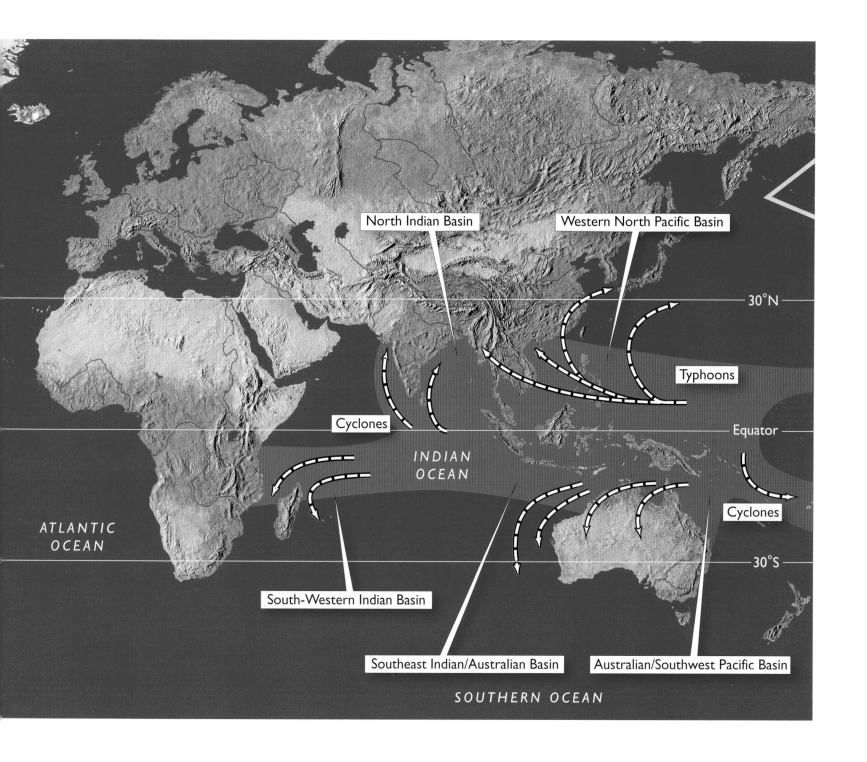

North Indian Basin

Western North Pacific Basin

30°N

Typhoons

Cyclones

Equator

INDIAN
OCEAN

ATLANTIC
OCEAN

Cyclones

South-Western Indian Basin

30°S

Southeast Indian/Australian Basin

Australian/Southwest Pacific Basin

SOUTHERN OCEAN

The 1970 Bay of Bengal storm is not the only tropical cyclone that helped determine the fate of a nation. The Japanese credit two thirteenth century storms with helping their country maintain its independence. Storms that sunk invasion-fleet ships, killing thousands of solders thwarted attempts by Kublai Khan, whose empire stretched from Europe to Korea, to invade Japan, in 1274 and again in 1281. The 1274 storm could have been a typhoon, which is a northwestern Pacific tropical cyclone. The 1281 storm, which killed an estimated 100,000 of Kublai Khan's 150,000 invaders, was surely a typhoon. The Japanese called these storms kamikazes, which means divine winds.

Hurricane Katrina's storm surge washes into Gulfport, Mississippi, on August 29, 2005.

Typhoons are tropical cyclones over the northern Pacific Ocean west of the International Date Line. This basin averages by far the greatest number of tropical cyclones of any other basin because the large, warm ocean allows more storms to grow. Unlike in the other basins, there is no official typhoon season because they have occurred in every month of the year, but the largest number do occur from May through November.

Typhoons that form over the vast Pacific Ocean threaten not only small islands, such as Truk, but also the heavily populated nations of Japan, Korea, China, Taiwan, the Philippines, and Vietnam, with some of the worst destruction and highest death tolls occurring in the Philippines. Even though typhoons are often deadly and destructive, they also bring needed rain to the nations they hit.

When satellites first began keeping track of tropical cyclones in the late 1950s, meteorologists discovered that roughly twice as many storms as they thought occurred over the Pacific Ocean north of the equator and east of the Date Line. This is easy to understand. Fewer ships cross this ocean than the Atlantic and most of the storms, including some strong hurricanes, form off the coasts of Mexico or Central America and head west to die over the empty ocean.

A few hurricanes curve back to the north and east to hit Mexico's Pacific Coast, occasionally doing serious damage to resort areas such as Acapulco. The remnants of the storms can move into California, the U.S. Southwest – making the deserts bloom – and even as far east as Oklahoma with flooding rain.

Hurricane Dennis blows over power line poles in Cienfuegos, Cuba on July 8, 2005.

The only hurricane known to ever have hit the U.S. West Coast occurred on October 2, 1858 when a Category 1 hurricane or a strong tropical storm brushed San Diego, California. The eye seemed to have stayed offshore, but a surgeon at a U.S. Army fort in San Diego measured hurricane-force wind gusts. Heavy rain and winds caused damage from San Diego to Los Angeles. A tropical storm hit Long Beach in late September 1939 with 50 mph winds.

A few eastern Pacific hurricanes brush or even hit Hawaii, but these are extremely rare. Also rare are storms that form in the central Pacific south of Hawaii and move north to hit the state. But, Hawaii's most devastating hurricane, Iniki, moved toward the north to strike the Hawaiian Island of Kauai on Sept. 10-11, 1992 killing six people and doing $2.3 billion damage, including to the world-famous Poipu resort district.

Tropical cyclones also hit Australia's northeast, north, and northwest coasts, but since most of the coasts, except for Queensland in the northeast, are not heavily populated, Australian cyclones have done limited damage compared with tropical cyclones elsewhere in the world.

Australia's deadliest cyclone was the one that hit Bathurst Bay in Queensland in March 1899, killing 307 people, mostly on pearl-fishing boats. The nation's costliest cyclone leveled the city of Darwin on Christmas Day 1974. It killed sixty-five people and destroyed more than 6,300 of the city's 9,000 houses.

Until March 2004 a hurricane had never been reported in the Atlantic Ocean south of the equator, although meteorologists had spotted a couple of what looked like tropical storms in satellite images. Then, on March 28, 2004 a hurricane, which had been seen in satellite images and identified by U.S. National Hurricane Center hurricane specialists, hit the Brazilian state of Santa Catarina, killing at least three people and leaving more than 2,000 homeless.

The global nature of tropical cyclones means that anyone who is planning a visit to a tropical location should look into whether or not hurricanes occur in the location and if so what time of the year such a storm is most likely.

Hurricane Douglas over the eastern Pacific west of Mexico on July 23, 2002. Like most eastern Pacific hurricanes, it moved west to die over the ocean without ever hitting land.

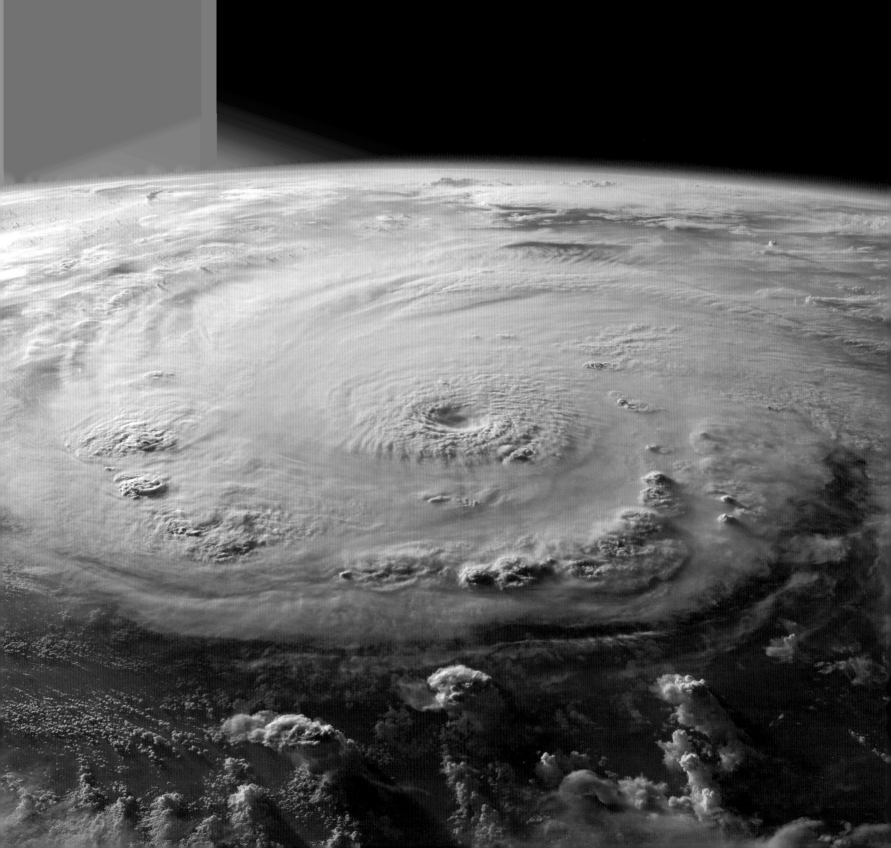

Climate Change and Hurricanes

The four hurricanes that hit Florida in 2004, followed, by the record-breaking 2005 hurricane season with three of the most-intense storms on record – Katrina, Rita, and Wilma – made Americans aware that hurricane seasons had become unusually active; at least compared with recent decades.

The unbelievable devastation of New Orleans by Katrina in 2005, along with some highly publicized articles that argued global warming caused increased numbers of intense tropical cyclones, convinced many commentators and the public of this inevitability. Surveys show that 75 percent of Americans who are concerned about global warming believe it will cause more and stronger hurricanes.

Atmospheric scientists contend that global warming is not responsible for any particular storm, including Hurricane Katrina. In the wake of the 2004-5 hurricane seasons, many of those who were convinced that their unusual frequency and intensity was caused by global warming, faced a problem with the 2006 season. No hurricanes struck the US in that year, and it had below average storms – with only nine tropical storms forming (eleven is average), five that became hurricanes (six is average), and two that grew to category 3 (two is average). There is current scientific debate regarding a possible relationship between global warming and more powerful hurricanes. Some modelling studies indicate that even if global warming could cause more intense storms, that shearing winds may also be enhanced, which would serve to lower their strength before making landfall. The jury is still out on this issue.

An El Niño is probably the main reason for a relatively quiet hurricane season in 2006. The term 'El Niño' is shorthand for a complex set of oceanic and atmospheric conditions characterized by warming of the water in the central and eastern tropical

International Space Station photo of Hurricane Felix over the Caribbean Sea in 2007.

Pacific Ocean. One of El Niño's effects is an increase in upper atmospheric winds blowing from the west across the Caribbean and tropical Atlantic. Such winds tend to shear apart storms.

Scientists also noted that during 2006, the steering winds around the Bermuda High kept the four long-lasting hurricanes far out in the Atlantic. The fifth weakened to a tropical storm before hitting Cuba and the United States. Winds across the tropical Atlantic were stronger than usual, which stirred up the ocean, bringing up cool water to slightly cool the ocean's surface temperature. Some scientists believe that dry, dusty air from over Africa's Sahara Desert 'contaminated' several fledgling storm systems off the African Coast, keeping them from growing.

The number of factors that could have contributed to the rather mild 2006 season helps illustrate why atmospheric scientists do not like to ascribe weather events such as hurricanes or heat waves to any one cause. Factors ranging from global patterns to small-scale disturbances help determine where and when a hurricane or any other storm forms. The most that can be said is that something like El Niño or global warming can decrease or increase the odds of a hurricane forming or growing stronger. Such effects would be seen over the long term, not in the case of any particular storm.

One of the best sources of the latest, considered thinking of the majority of climate scientists is the report issued in February 2007 by Working Group 1 of the Intergovernmental Panel on Climate Change (IPCC). In its 2007 report, the IPCC stated there is 'very high confidence' that both the gases that humans have emitted into the atmosphere and changes in land use have caused the global climate to warm since the 18th century, with the gases playing by far the major role in warming.

The IPCC report reflects the general agreement by climate scientists that greenhouse gases that humans are adding to the air are causing a big part of this warming. Greenhouse gases are those such as carbon dioxide and water vapor that are warmed when they absorb infrared heat emitted by the Earth. The gases then radiate infrared heat of their own in all directions, including toward the ground. Without greenhouse gases; life as we know it would not exist on Earth because the global average temperature at the surface would be close to 0 degrees Fahrenheit (-19° C) instead of the current 60 degrees F (15° C). Today's concern is about the enhanced greenhouse effect caused by carbon dioxide being added by burning fossil fuels and other greenhouse gases such as methane and nitrous oxide from human activities.

The oceans have been absorbing most of the heat added to the climate system. It seems logical that a warmer world will produce more powerful hurricanes because warm oceans supply the energy for hurricanes, and warmer water is one of the factors that can cause a hurricane to strengthen. In fact, some computer models show that peak wind speeds and peak rainfall intensity of tropical storms should increase in a warmer world.

One major complication is that climate changes on three different time scales affect Atlantic Basin hurricanes, especially the number of intense storms. These are:

- El Niño and its opposite, La Niña, (a cooling of central and eastern Pacific water), which comes and goes in a three- to seven- year cycle.

- The Atlantic Multidecadal Oscillation (AMO), a slight warming and cooling of the Atlantic Ocean with a 20- to 40-year cycle.

- Global warming, which has many effects other than warming temperatures, and is normally measured in many hundreds to thousands of years.

While an El Niño tends to reduce the number of strong hurricanes, La Niña tends to increase them. But, coastal residents cannot count on El Niño for protection. A weak El Niño in 1992 held that year's activity down to seven tropical storms with only four becoming hurricanes. Three of those hurricanes never threatened land. The fourth was Category 5 Hurricane Andrew, which until Katrina was the most expensive U.S. disaster.

The AMO is characterized by a warm and a cool phase of Atlantic Ocean temperatures, each of which can last 20 to 40 years. The temperature change is only approximately 1 degree Fahrenheit (half a degree Celsius). This does not seem like much, but the amount of energy available to tropical systems is significant over the entire Atlantic basin.

Many hurricane scientists are convinced that the AMO cycle accounts for the few major hurricanes that formed from 1970 through 1994, and the many that have formed since 1995 – with wide year-to-year variations caused by the El Niño-Southern Oscillation (ENSO) cycle and random chance. Regardless of the reason for the large numbers of intense hurricanes since 1995, this makes one pause and consider seriously the possible adverse impacts in terms of more powerful storms and future hurricane disasters.

We should bear in mind that human decisions may pose as big a problem as the climate can. In July 2006 hurricane and climate scientists on different sides of the debate over global warming and hurricanes concluded that the United States' main hurricane problem is the ever-growing concentration of population and wealth in vulnerable coastal regions. Rapidly escalating hurricane damage in recent decades is directly linked to policies that serve to subsidize risk. State regulation of insurance is captive to political pressures that hold down premiums in risky coastal areas at the expense of higher premiums for the general populace. U.S. flood insurance programs likewise undercharge property owners in vulnerable areas. Federal disaster policies, while providing obvious humanitarian benefits, paradoxically reward risky behavior in the long run.

To avoid future disasters such as Katrina, local, state, and the national governments need to undertake a comprehensive evaluation of building practices, land use, insurance, and disaster relief policies that currently serve to promote an ever-increasing vulnerability to hurricanes.

Debris litters part of Gulfport, Mississippi, in the wake of Hurricane Katrina in 2005.

Glossary

AMO: the Atlantic multi-decadal oscillation is a 20 to 40 year cycle that results in surface water temperatures shifts between warm and cool that greatly influence the energy available for tropical storms; the shift to warmer water occurred in 1995, which is denoted by a marked increase in the number of Atlantic hurricanes since that time.

Bermuda High: A large area of high atmospheric pressure centered on approximately 30 degrees north latitude in the central and western Atlantic Ocean. Its exact location and size vary and help control the paths of hurricanes moving across the Atlantic.

Cyclone: An area of low atmospheric pressure at the Earth's surface with wind making a complete circle around the low pressure moving counterclockwise (as viewed from above) in the Northern Hemisphere, and clockwise in the Southern Hemisphere. 'Cyclone' is also used to refer to a tropical cyclone in the Indian and South Pacific oceans.

El Niño: An anomalous warming of surface water of the eastern, tropical Pacific and cooling of the surface water in the western Pacific. These changes affect global weather patterns that include a reduction in the number of Atlantic hurricanes. In popular use, El Niño often refers to all atmospheric and oceanic events connected to the changes in Pacific Ocean temperatures.

Eye: The center of a strong tropical cyclone, which is the location of the storm's lowest surface atmospheric pressure. The eye is often cloud free or nearly cloud free.

Eye Wall: The wall of thunderstorms surrounding a tropical cyclone's eye; usually the location of the storm's strongest winds.

Forecast Cone of Uncertainty: A generally cone shaped area on hurricane forecast maps produced by the U.S. National Hurricane Center and many news media outlets. The cone shows the area with 66% chance of being traversed by the storm's eye.

High Pressure: An area with atmospheric pressures that are higher than those of surrounding areas. Generally associated with fair weather.

Hurricane: A tropical cyclone with sustained winds of 74 mph (119 km/hour) or faster occurring over the Atlantic Ocean, the Caribbean Sea, the Gulf of Mexico, or the Pacific Ocean north of the equator and east of the International Date Line.

Hurricane Force Wind: A sustained wind of 74 mph (119 km/hour) or faster. Hurricane-force winds can occur in any kind of storm.

Hurricane Season: From June 1 through November 30 in the Atlantic Basin, when almost all hurricanes occur.

International Hurricane Research Center (IHRC): A multi-disciplinary research and education center at the Florida International University in Miami. The IHRC's mission is to lower and prevent damage from hurricanes, to make coastal communities less vulnerable to hurricane impact, and to assist communities in the aftermath of land falling events.

La Niña: A collection of oceanic and atmospheric phenomena that in many ways are opposite of El Niño, including increased chances of more Atlantic hurricanes.

Low Pressure: An area where the atmospheric pressure is lower than surrounding pressures. Generally associated with clouds and precipitation.

National Hurricane Center (NHC): One of the NWS' major forecasting centers. It has the responsibility of monitoring and forecasting tropical cyclones in the Atlantic and Northeast Pacific basin east of 140 degrees west longitude.

National Weather Service (NWS): The U.S. National Weather Service has responsibility for public forecasting. Its parent agency is the National Oceanic and Atmospheric Administration, a part of the Cabinet-level Department of Commerce.

Rain Bands: Long, narrow lines of thunderstorms, which are oriented in the same direction as the horizontal winds, that spiral into the center of a tropical cyclone to form the eye wall.

Storm Surge: The mound of water that builds up on the right, front side of a tropical cyclone's eye wall and which causes a rapid rise of water when the storm comes ashore.

Tropical Cyclone: A cyclone that forms over a warm tropical or subtropical ocean.

Tropical Depression: A tropical cyclone with winds slower than 39 mph (63 km/hour).

Tropical Storm: A tropical cyclone with winds faster then 39 mph (63 km/hour) and slower than 74 mph (119 km/hour)

Typhoon: A tropical cyclone with sustained winds of 74 mph (119 km/hour) or faster occurring over the Pacific Ocean north of the equator and west of the International Date Line.

Wind Rolls: A rolling motion of a tropical cyclone's winds that begin when it moves over land. They bring down high-speed air from just above the ground down to smash into the ground causing streaks of damage caused by some storms. The bursts slow down before being carried aloft on the opposite side of the roll where they re-strengthen and slam downward again.

Wind Shear: A change in wind speed or direction in a local area. Such shear created by winds at different levels of the atmosphere from the ocean to higher than 40,000 feet can tear apart a tropical cyclone, or keep a tropical cyclone from growing.

World Meteorological Organization (WMO): The WMO is a specialized agency of the United Nations and is the UN system's authoritative voice on the state and behavior of the Earth's atmosphere. It promotes cooperation in weather observations among its 118 member nations and assists technology transfer, training and research.

Index (Entries in **bold** indicate pictures)

Recommended Reading & Useful Websites

Emanuel, Kerry, *Divine Wind: The History and Science of Hurricanes*, Oxford University Press, USA, 2005

Larson, Erik, *Isaac's Storm: A Man, a Time, and the Deadliest Hurricane in History*, Vintage, 2000

Norcross, Bryan *Hurricane Almanac: The Essential Guide to Storms Past, Present, and Future*, St. Martin's Griffin, 2007

Sheets, Bob and Williams, Jack, *Hurricane Watch: Forecasting the Deadliest Storms on Earth*, Vintage 2001

U.S. National Hurricane Center:
http://www.nhc.noaa.gov/index.shtml

International Hurricane Research Center:
http://www.ihrc.fiu.edu/

Weather Underground:
http://www.wunderground.com

NOAA FAQ about hurricanes, cyclones, and typhoons: http://www.aoml.noaa.gov/hrd/tcfaq/tcfaqHED.html

UNISYS Global Tropical Cyclone Archive: http://weather.unisys.com/hurricane/index.html

Eastern Long Island Coastal Conservation Alliance: http://www.elicca.org

Biographical Notes

Dr. Stephen P. Leatherman is Director of the International Hurricane Research Center at Florida International University. He is author of over 16 books and National Academy of Science reports along with hundreds of scientific articles and papers, and several popular books, including *America's Best Beaches* for University Press of Florida as well as beach books for AAA and Yale University Press.

Jack Williams has been public outreach coordinator for the American Meteorological Society (AMS) since April 2005. He was the founding editor of the USA Today weather page in 1982, and is the author of the *USA Today Weather Book*, The *USA Today Weather Almanac*, and co-author of *Hurricane Watch: Forecasting the Deadliest Storms on Earth*. He also wrote *The Complete Idiots Guide to the Arctic and Antarctic*.